LITTLE RABBITS

GRAY RABBIT'S
123

ALAN BAKER

KINGFISHER
NEW YORK

KINGFISHER
LONDON & NEW YORK

First published 1994 by Kingfisher
This edition published 2017 by Kingfisher
Published in the United States by Kingfisher,
175 Fifth Ave., New York, NY 10010
Kingfisher is an imprint of Macmillan Children's Books, London.
All rights reserved.

Copyright © Alan Baker 1994

Distributed in the U.S. and Canada by Macmillan,
175 Fifth Ave., New York, NY 10010

Library of Congress Cataloging-in-Publication data
has been applied for.

ISBN: 978-0-7534-7324-5 (HB)
ISBN: 978-0-7534-7325-2 (PB)

Kingfisher books are available for special promotions
and premiums. For details contact: Special Markets
Department, Macmillan, 175 Fifth Ave.,
New York, NY 10010.

For more information, please visit
www.kingfisherbooks.com

Printed in China
9 8 7 6 5 4 3 2 1
1TR/1116/WKT/UG/157MA

One day Gray Rabbit
found some clay.

He made one
wiggly,
squiggly

worm,

two
chattering,
clattering

toucans,

three
growling,
prowling

bears,

3

four happy, yappy

dogs,

five
freckled,
speckled

frogs,

six
sliding,
gliding

snakes,

seven
so slow

snails,

eight
rumpeting,
trumpeting

elephants,

nine
spotted,
dotted

bugs,

9

and ten
squeaking,
peeking

mice,

10

which left
at the end
of the day
one
weary,
bleary

rabbit fast asleep.

E BAKER
Baker, Alan,
Gray Rabbit's 1, 2, 3 /

FLT

05/17